26161553

"It was not for their own land they fought, nor even for a land which had adopted them, but for a land which had enslaved them. . . . Bravery, under such circumstances, has a peculiar beauty and merit."

— HARRIET BEECHER STOWE
in COLORED PATRIOTS OF THE AMERICAN REVOLUTION

African Americans and the Revolutionary War

By Judith E. Harper

The Child's World

GRAPHIC DESIGN
Robert E. Bonaker / Graphic Design & Consulting Co.

PROJECT COORDINATOR
James R. Rothaus / James R. Rothaus & Associates

EDITORIAL DIRECTION
Elizabeth Sirimarco Budd

COVER PHOTO
Colonial actor fires a musket
©Raymond Gehman/CORBIS

Library of Congress Cataloging-in-Publication Data
Harper, Judith E., 1953–
African Americans and the Revolutionary War / by Judith E. Harper.
p. cm.
Includes bibliographical references (p. 40) and index.
Summary: Portrays the treatment and struggles of African
Americans during the Revolutionary War and their
contributions to the war effort.
ISBN 1-56766-745-7 (lib. bdg. : alk. paper)

1. United States — History — Revolution, 1775–1783 — Afro-
Americans — Juvenile literature. 2. United States — History —
Revolution, 1775–1783 — Participation, Afro-American — Juvenile
literature. 3. Afro-Americans — History — 18th century — Juvenile
literature. [1. United States — History — Revolution, 1775–1783 —
Afro-Americans. 2. Afro-Americans — History — To 1863.] I. Title

E269.N3 H37 2000
973.3'08996073 — dc21

00-021400

Contents

African Americans and the Struggle for Freedom

It was Christmas Day, 1776. The wind howled. An icy rain fell from gray clouds. General George Washington stood on the banks of the Delaware River in Pennsylvania. He was desperate. He knew his soldiers must win the next battle against the British. One more defeat, and his army would give up the fight and go home.

Twenty thousand soldiers had marched with Washington during the past year. But now, most had returned to their farms and their families. Only about 2,400 remained. These soldiers were strong and loyal. But they were also starving, cold, and sick. If they left the army, the **War for Independence** would be over. The dream of an **independent** American nation would be lost. The British would still rule the American colonies.

An African slave named Prince Whipple was one soldier who did not give up. He was the bodyguard of General William Whipple, General Washington's **aide.** On that wintry Christmas Night, Prince Whipple helped row Washington's army across the Delaware River.

The next morning, the Americans launched a surprise attack on **Hessian** troops at Trenton, New Jersey. The Hessians were fighting for the British. These Hessian soldiers were sleepy from their Christmas celebrations. They did not have a chance to fight back when the Americans arrived. With the Battle of Trenton, Washington's army had a victory at last!

Prince Whipple earned his freedom by serving in the army. So did most slaves who joined the American military. But not all those who served became free. At the end of the war, some slave owners forced their slaves to return to slavery.

PRINCE WHIPPLE IS SEEN AT THE FRONT OF GENERAL WASHINGTON'S BOAT AS IT CROSSES THE DELAWARE RIVER. WHIPPLE WAS BORN IN THE AFRICAN VILLAGE OF AMABOU. HIS WEALTHY FATHER SENT HIM TO AMERICA WHEN HE WAS 10 YEARS OLD. HE WANTED HIS SON TO RECEIVE AN EXCELLENT EDUCATION. WHEN PRINCE'S BOAT DOCKED IN AMERICA, THE CAPTAIN OF THE SHIP SEIZED THE BOY. HE SOLD PRINCE INTO SLAVERY. PRINCE REMAINED A SLAVE UNTIL THE REVOLUTIONARY WAR GAVE HIM A CHANCE TO EARN HIS FREEDOM.

©Bettmann/CORBIS

BRITISH SOLDIERS SHOOT CRISPUS ATTUCKS, AN UNARMED AFRICAN AMERICAN PATRIOT, DURING THE BOSTON MASSACRE. ATTUCKS WAS ONE OF THE FIRST PEOPLE KILLED IN THE REVOLUTION.

At least 5,000 **African American** men and boys served in the American army during the Revolutionary War. Some were free, but most were slaves. Black soldiers were present at every important battle of the war. They were there when the first shot was fired at the Battle of Lexington and Concord. They survived the cold and hunger at Valley Forge. They helped force the British to surrender at Yorktown. African American women and girls were there, too. They worked in the army camps and helped keep the soldiers alive. When the army moved, they walked right along behind the soldiers.

Some African American women helped without leaving their communities. Lucretia Emmons, a young slave woman, lived in New Jersey. She worked in the home of Captain Huddy, a **patriot.** One day, an angry mob of **Loyalists** appeared. They attacked the Huddy home. Lucretia knew that she and the captain were in terrible danger. She also knew they had to fight back. Quickly and carefully, she loaded and reloaded the captain's **muskets.** This helped him fire the guns more rapidly. The Loyalists then set fire to the house. Luckily, a band of patriots rescued Lucretia and the captain.

During the Revolutionary War, there were about 2.5 million people living in America. About 500,000 of them were slaves. In other words, about one out of every five people in America was owned by another American. Almost all slaves were born in Africa or were of African **descent.** A few thousand were Native Americans.

Most of the slaves lived in the South. They worked on large farms called plantations. The white owners of these plantations forced their slaves to farm the crops for them. Slaves had terribly hard lives. They worked in the fields from dawn until after dark. Plantation owners gave them barely enough food to survive. Slave shelters were tiny and drafty. They leaked when it rained and were not heated in winter.

There were also slaves in the North and in the middle colonies, but not nearly so many. Their owners had them work at all kinds of jobs, not just farming. No matter where slaves lived, they all dreamed of freedom.

Not all black people in America were slaves. Every colony had some free black people. There were about 40,000 free black men, women, and children scattered all over America at the beginning of the Revolutionary War. Many were either the children or the grandchildren of slaves. Others had once been slaves themselves. These free African Americans were very poor. Adults and children had to work long hours to earn enough money to stay alive. But they had their freedom.

Freedom was won in other places besides the battlefield. In Massachusetts, a few slaves gained their liberty before the war. They went to court to prove that they were free people. These court cases were called "freedom suits." Most of the people who filed them succeeded in becoming free.

Jenny Slew was a free African American woman. She went to court because a man **seized** her and forced her to be his slave. She failed to win her first case. But she did not give up. She insisted that the court try her case again. This time a jury declared her to be a free woman.

In 1773, a group of slaves from Massachusetts sent a **petition** to the General Court. These men explained why they wanted their freedom. "We have no property! We have no wives! We have no children! No city! No country!" they said. White leaders discussed their plea but refused their request. This was the first of many freedom petitions.

PHILLIS WHEATLEY WAS A GREAT POET. SHE WAS BORN
IN AFRICA AND WAS BROUGHT TO AMERICA AS A SLAVE.
SHE WAS SO GIFTED WITH WORDS THAT HER OWNERS
TAUGHT HER TO READ AND WRITE. AT AGE 17,
WHEATLEY BECAME THE FIRST BLACK WOMAN TO HAVE
A BOOK OF POETRY PUBLISHED. SHE WROTE PATRIOTIC
POEMS DURING THE REVOLUTIONARY WAR. SHE EVEN
WROTE ONE FOR GENERAL GEORGE WASHINGTON.

African American Minutemen

In the spring of 1775, the villages and towns of Massachusetts were buzzing with activity. The American colonists were fed up with British rule. They wanted freedom from British **tyranny.** White and black men formed **militias.** They prepared to fight the British. These soldiers were called **minutemen** because they promised to fight at a minute's notice. Early on the morning of April 19, the British marched toward the town of Concord. They planned to seize the patriots' military supplies. The minutemen rushed to defend their property.

Peter Salem is probably the best known of all the African American minutemen. He was a slave who lived about 15 miles from Concord. His owners, the Belknap family, gave him his freedom so that he could join the minutemen. He fought at the Battle of Lexington and Concord. But he is better known for his actions at the Battle of Bunker Hill.

The Battle of Bunker Hill came two months after Lexington and Concord. The minutemen were determined to force the British army and navy to leave Boston. On the night of June 16, 1775, they prepared for a battle on top of Breed's Hill. This hill and Bunker Hill overlooked all the British ships in Boston Harbor.

All night, black and white minutemen made a structure out of earth. These **earthworks** were like a huge wall. They were tall, but they were also dug deep into the ground. They protected the minutemen as they attacked the British.

The next afternoon, on June 17, the British charged up Breed's Hill. When they came close to the earthworks, the minutemen opened fire. They killed and wounded many British soldiers in that first attack. The British had no choice but to **retreat** down the hill. They tried to attack the earthworks a second time. Once again the minutemen's guns forced them back.

©Francis G. Mayer/CORBIS

JOHN TRUMBULL'S PAINTING *THE BATTLE OF BUNKER HILL* HELPED MAKE PETER SALEM, SHOWN IN THE FAR RIGHT CORNER, A FAMOUS HERO. MANY HISTORIANS THINK THAT HE PROBABLY DID NOT KILL BRITISH MAJOR JOHN PITCAIRN. THE AIR THAT DAY WAS FILLED WITH SMOKE, DUST, AND NOISE. THERE WAS NO WAY TO KNOW WHO FIRED THAT SHOT. EVEN SO, THE STORIES AND THIS PAINTING ARE STILL IMPORTANT. THEY SHOW THAT AFRICAN AMERICAN SOLDIERS WERE FIGHTING EARLY IN THE WAR.

After the second attack, the minutemen faced disaster: they had no more gunpowder. The British stormed the earthworks a third time. Now there was nothing to hold them back. They captured Breed's Hill and Bunker Hill. British Major John Pitcairn leapt on top of the earthworks. He shouted, "The day is ours!" According to stories told after the battle, Peter Salem had some **ammunition** left. He shot and killed Pitcairn.

A strange thing happened in the months after the Battle of Bunker Hill. Army officers prevented black soldiers from enlisting. When Washington was gathering soldiers for his army, he was told to exclude black men. African Americans could not understand this. Why should they be turned away? Hadn't they fought bravely all through 1775?

There were a number of reasons for this new policy. White slave owners were complaining to the government. They did not want their slaves to become free by joining the army. They said that the government should respect their rights to their "property." The government agreed.

White leaders and slave owners were also afraid to give guns to slaves. They feared that the slaves would use guns to start a **rebellion.** Perhaps they would free all the slaves. This would mean the end of slavery.

By December 1776, Washington and other generals had to change their policy. Thousands of white soldiers had left the army. There were too few men to make a strong fighting force. To make matters worse, the British were enlisting slaves and free black men. The British promised freedom to any black soldier who joined them. The American army could not afford to grow weaker while the British became stronger. Ever so slowly, the American military let African American soldiers sign up.

Contributors To The Cause...

U.S. 10c

©David M. Budd Photography

Salem Poor ✿ Gallant Soldier

A BLACK MINUTEMAN NAMED SALEM POOR FOUGHT SO BRAVELY AT THE BATTLE OF BUNKER HILL THAT 14 WHITE OFFICERS HONORED HIS HEROISM. THEY SIGNED A PETITION AND SENT IT TO THE GENERAL COURT IN MASSACHUSETTS. IT SAID THAT SALEM POOR "BEHAVED LIKE AN EXPERIENCED OFFICER, AS WELL AS AN EXCELLENT SOLDIER." IN 1975, 200 YEARS AFTER THE BATTLE OF BUNKER HILL, THE UNITED STATES POSTAL SERVICE ISSUED THIS POSTAGE STAMP. IT CELEBRATES SALEM POOR'S COURAGE.

Stockbridge Library Association Historical Collection

AGRIPPA HULL WAS A FREE-BORN MASSACHUSETTS MAN. HE WAS AN ORDERLY IN THE AMERICAN ARMY. HE FOUGHT IN A NUMBER OF MAJOR BATTLES. AFTER THE WAR, HE RETURNED HOME. HE AND HIS WIFE ADOPTED A SLAVE GIRL WHO HAD ESCAPED TO FREEDOM.

In the Army

Most African American military men were poor. Those who were slaves had nothing at all. Free black men often joined the army because they needed the wages and food **rations** to survive. The ordinary black soldier was a **private** of the lowest rank. Almost all black soldiers served in the **infantry.** A few worked in **artillery.** Most African Americans worked at jobs that white soldiers did not want to do.

Black soldiers had important jobs before a battle. They cut down trees to block the enemy from moving forward. They tore down bridges that the British wanted to cross. They built structures to protect the American army from gun and cannon fire. They also served as **orderlies,** messengers, cooks, waiters, and servants to officers. They drove and repaired the wagons. They cared for the horses. And, during battles, they fought.

Many African American soldiers brought their wives and children with them to the army camps. Poor white soldiers had their families with them, too. These men had no choice. Their families could not earn enough to live back home. These women and children worked hard for the army.

About 20,000 white and African American women worked for the American army. Women and girls washed the clothing of the officers and soldiers. They sewed and mended coats, underwear, and socks. This was important work because the army did not have money for new uniforms.

Women and girls cooked for the troops. They also nursed the wounded and sick soldiers. This, too, was an important job. Disease and injury were common. The nurses helped the soldiers survive their wounds and their sicknesses.

Women were also important during times of battle. They carried gunpowder to the men loading the cannons. They carried pails of water to cool the guns. They made bullets and prepared other ammunition.

For all this work, a woman received half a soldier's food ration. Sometimes she earned a small wage, too. Children were often given only one quarter of a soldier's ration. For many, this was not enough food.

Historians believe that several hundred women became soldiers in the American armies. To do this, the women dressed in men's clothing and pretended to be men. The names of some of these women are known — all of them white. It is likely that at least a few black women were soldiers, too.

Both African American men and women were spies. James Armistead is the best known of the African American spies. He was a slave on a farm near Williamsburg, Virginia. In 1781, his owner allowed him to serve the Marquis de Lafayette, a French general in the Continental Army. Lafayette sent Armistead to spy on the British.

Armistead proved to be a top-notch spy. He went to a British camp and pretended to be just another black worker. He was quiet. He did not call any attention to himself. As a result, he was able to listen in on many conversations. He gathered facts about the British troops and their plans. He sent the details to Lafayette.

On one important mission, Lafayette sent Armistead to the camp of Lord Cornwallis, the commander of the British forces in the South. Armistead soon landed a job working in the tent of Cornwallis himself! Armistead felt so lucky. There he was — surrounded by maps, papers, and plans. Surely he would learn Cornwallis's top secrets! But Cornwallis guarded his papers very carefully.

National Archives

LAFAYETTE (AT LEFT) SENT JAMES ARMISTEAD (RIGHT) TO SPY ON LORD CORNWALLIS. AFTER THE SURRENDER OF THE BRITISH AT YORKTOWN, LORD CORNWALLIS HAD A MEETING WITH LAFAYETTE. CORNWALLIS WAS SHOCKED TO FIND JAMES ARMISTEAD WORKING FOR LAFAYETTE. AFTER ALL, ARMISTEAD HAD BEEN CORNWALLIS'S SPY — OR SO HE HAD THOUGHT. ARMISTEAD HAD FOOLED CORNWALLIS COMPLETELY!

It was a frustrating time for Armistead. He kept his eyes and ears open. He waited and collected all the facts he could. Then Cornwallis sent Armistead to spy on Lafayette! This made it easier for Armistead to deliver messages to Lafayette. Armistead told Lafayette every move that the British army and navy made.

In the fall of 1781, Armistead told Lafayette that the British were gathering their ships along the York River in Virginia. Washington had been waiting for this information. Finally the Americans would be able to trap the British. They would do this near the village of Yorktown in Virginia. Total victory for the Americans was now within reach!

African American boys were heroes, too. They served with men in the American army and navy. One boy who served in both the army and the navy was James Forten.

One day in 1775, nine-year-old James was working in the grocery store near his home. James was a free African American living in the city of Philadelphia. He heard men talking about General Washington and his army. James listened eagerly. How he wished he could be a part of the American struggle for freedom!

When James went home, he begged his mother to let him join the soldiers. His mother insisted that he wait until he was older. She reminded him that his family needed him. Ever since his father had died, times had been hard for the Fortens.

Valentine Museum, Richmond, Virginia

AFTER THE WAR, JAMES ARMISTEAD CALLED HIMSELF
JAMES ARMISTEAD LAFAYETTE, IN HONOR OF THE FRENCH
GENERAL. UNFORTUNATELY, ARMISTEAD WAS FORCED TO
RETURN TO SLAVERY. LAFAYETTE TRIED TO PERSUADE
VIRGINIA LEADERS TO GIVE ARMISTEAD HIS FREEDOM.

In 1777, when James was 11, he could wait no longer. He became a drummer boy in a militia unit for a short time. Four years later, he signed up to be a powder boy on a ship named the *Royal Louis*.

The colony of Pennsylvania ordered the *Royal Louis*, a **privateer,** to go to sea. Its mission was to seize the cargo of British **merchant ships.** As a powder boy, James had many duties. During battle, his job was to carry gunpowder to the guns and cannons. This was extremely dangerous work.

Soon after setting sail, the *Royal Louis* saw its first combat. It was a tough, bloody battle. James was in danger every minute. He carried gunpowder and cannonballs to the artillery crew. Explosions boomed all around him. The *Royal Louis* captured a British merchant ship.

The next time the *Royal Louis* met the enemy, it was not so lucky. Three British warships overpowered the American privateer. The *Royal Louis* was seized by one of them, the *Amphyon*.

As an African American, James knew he was in terrible danger. He was born free, but the British did not know that, nor did they care. The British navy usually put white American sailors in prison. They sold black sailors into slavery in the **West Indies.**

James became friendly with the son of the *Amphyon's* captain. This British boy was amazed by how well James could play marbles. The captain's son convinced his father to let James return with them to England. James refused the invitation. He told them, "I am here a prisoner for the liberties of my country; I never, never shall prove a **traitor** to her interests!"

The Historical Society of Pennsylvania

JAMES FORTEN GREW UP TO BECOME A FAMOUS AMERICAN. HE INVENTED A NEW WAY TO RAISE SAILS ON SHIPS. HE OWNED A SAIL-MAKING COMPANY AND BECAME WEALTHY. DURING THE EARLY 1800s, HE WORKED TO CONVINCE WHITE AMERICANS TO PASS LAWS OUTLAWING SLAVERY.

Fortunately, the captain did not sell James into slavery. He sent James to a British prison ship named the *Jersey*. The captain asked the commander of the *Jersey* to make James part of an exchange of prisoners. This eventually would make James free. An exchange of prisoners occurred when Britain and America would agree to swap a certain number of their prisoners. This allowed both countries to get back some of the soldiers they had lost.

Life on board the *Jersey* was pure misery for James. When he learned that an American officer was about to be exchanged, he had an idea. Why not hide himself in the officer's chest of belongings? What an excellent way to escape! But, at the last minute, he changed his mind. He let a younger boy who was very sick go in his place.

After seven months of suffering, there was an exchange of prisoners. James was finally set free. Ragged and without shoes, he walked home to his family in Philadelphia.

ELEVEN THOUSAND AMERICANS DIED ON THE BRITISH PRISON SHIP *JERSEY* DURING THE REVOLUTIONARY WAR. MOST DIED FROM DISEASE AND STARVATION.

For seven months, James Forten lived in the total darkness of the *Jersey's* hold. (The hold is the area within the hull of the ship. It is below the main deck.) A thousand men and boys were crammed into this space with James. There was very little food, and the few morsels they had were rotten and moldy. Lice and rats pestered the prisoners and spread diseases.

The War in the South

Not all African Americans fought for America during the Revolutionary War. In fact, most fought for the British. How did this happen?

In the South, wealthy plantation owners were the leaders of their colonies. When the war started, these slave owners did not want to fight the British. They knew that warfare would hurt or even destroy their crops. They would lose money.

Slave owners did not want their slaves to work for the American army. They needed the slaves to work in the fields. Without slave labor, they could not harvest their crops. At the same time, the English were promising slaves their freedom if they joined the British forces. Thousands of African Americans ran away from their owners, trusting that the British would later set them free.

THE BRITISH NEEDED MORE MEN AND WOMEN TO WORK FOR THEM. THEY PROMISED FREEDOM TO AMERICAN SLAVES IN EXCHANGE FOR THEIR HELP. MANY THOUSANDS OF SLAVES IN VIRGINIA, SOUTH CAROLINA, NORTH CAROLINA, AND GEORGIA RAN AWAY FROM THEIR OWNERS. THEY WANTED SO BADLY TO BE FREE THAT THEY WERE WILLING TO RISK THEIR LIVES.

Culver Pictures

Library of Congress

LIKE OTHER RICH LANDOWNERS IN VIRGINIA, GENERAL GEORGE
WASHINGTON OWNED MANY SLAVES. DURING THE WAR, HIS SLAVES
DEBORAH SQUASH AND HER HUSBAND HARRY RAN AWAY. THEY
FLED TO THE BRITISH, WHO HAD PROMISED THEM FREEDOM.

South Carolina State House; Sam Holland, photographer

NOT ALL AFRICAN AMERICANS IN THE SOUTH JOINED THE BRITISH. A FEW FOUGHT FOR THE AMERICANS. AT THE BATTLE OF COWPENS IN SOUTH CAROLINA, THIS YOUNG BLACK SOLDIER USED A REVOLVER BECAUSE HE WAS NOT TALL ENOUGH TO HANDLE A SWORD.

It was a dangerous time for all slaves in the South. When they fled to the British, they risked being captured by white Southerners. If the slaves were caught and returned to their owners, they were severely punished. Sometimes they were put to death.

The slaves who stayed on the plantations suffered, too. When the British army invaded the South, there was less food for everyone. Battles not only damaged crops, they also made it difficult to transport food to people. White slave owners often had just enough food to feed their families. They gave their slaves what little was left.

Without the proper amount of food, the slaves became weak and sick. The slave owners forced these tired, hungry slaves to do more work than before the war. They had to do their own work and the jobs of the runaway slaves, too.

The slave men, women, and children who joined the British were not safe either. The British forced them to work very hard for the army. When British food supplies ran low, they fed the slaves nothing but corn. Even when food was more plentiful, the slaves did not have enough to stay healthy. They died by the hundreds from serious illnesses.

Did the War Bring African Americans Their Freedom?

On October 19, 1781, the last battle of the Revolutionary War was fought. The Americans defeated the British at the Battle of Yorktown in Virginia. The British finally surrendered. Now the new American nation was free and independent. But what about the African American men and women who fought during the war? Did they gain the freedom they were promised?

Most African American slaves in the American army were free men by the end of the war. Many of their family members became free, too. But a number of slave owners forced their slaves to return to slavery.

What happened to the tens of thousands of slaves who served the British? Thousands died of disease during the war. Most of the survivors escaped to freedom with the British. Some sailed to new lives in Canada. Others went to Sierra Leone, a country in western Africa. Still others settled in Europe. But not all the African Americans who worked for the British received their freedom. Instead of beginning new lives as free people, some were sold to slave owners in the West Indies.

©Bettmann/CORBIS

THE BRITISH SURRENDERED TO THE AMERICANS AT YORKTOWN ON OCTOBER 19, 1781. BUT ALTHOUGH THE VICTORY GAINED MOST AMERICANS THEIR INDEPENDENCE, SLAVERY WAS STILL A TERRIBLE FACT OF LIFE IN THE NEW NATION.

Southern slave owners were furious that the British were taking their slaves. They demanded that the army and the government return their "property" to them. American leaders did everything they could to help the slave owners. But there was not much they could do. Only a small number of slaves were returned.

All during the war, white Northerners grew more certain that slavery was wrong. Both white and African American people tried to persuade their state governments to forbid slavery. Vermont leaders outlawed slavery in 1777. (At the time, Vermont was an independent republic. It did not enter the union and become a state until 1791.) In 1780, the leaders of Pennsylvania **abolished** slavery as well. Still, by 1790, only nine percent of all African Americans were free.

A slave woman in Massachusetts decided she could not wait for her state to pass such a law. Just as Jenny Slew had done back in 1766, Elizabeth Freeman sued for her freedom in 1781.

Elizabeth was a widow who had one daughter. Her husband had joined the American army to gain his freedom. But he was killed before he could enjoy it.

Elizabeth and her sister were servants in the home of Colonel Ashley. One day, the colonel's wife became angry. She tried to hit Elizabeth's sister with a shovel that was red-hot from the hearth. Elizabeth blocked the blow with her arm. Her arm was badly burned. Elizabeth was so fed up that she left the Ashleys. She promised herself she would never go back.

Colonel Ashley tried to force Elizabeth to return. She realized then that she needed a lawyer. She persuaded a man named Theodore Sedgwick to take her case. She told him that the new Massachusetts Bill of Rights said that all people are free and equal. She had learned about the Bill of Rights from discussions in Colonel Ashley's home. Sedgwick brought her case to trial. The jury agreed with Elizabeth. The court declared that she and her daughter were free.

Courtesy of the Massachusetts Historical Society

AFTER SHE WAS DECLARED FREE, ELIZABETH FREEMAN
WORKED AS A PAID SERVANT FOR THEODORE SEDGWICK,
THE LAWYER WHO HELPED WIN HER FREEDOM. HIS
DAUGHTER PAINTED THIS PORTRAIT OF HER.

By the early 1800s, slavery was no longer legal in most northern states. But the leaders of the new United States did not agree with many Northerners that slavery was wrong. They believed — just as the writers of the Declaration of Independence and the Constitution had — that the property rights of slave owners must be protected. Slavery would be a terrible reality in America for years to come.

The Revolutionary War brought some African Americans their freedom. But millions more were forced to remain slaves. Not until after the end of another war — the Civil War — would all African Americans in the United States be free. In 1865, the 13th **Amendment** to the Constitution became law. This amendment guaranteed the freedom of African Americans forever.

©Bettmann/CORBIS

CITIZENS OF BOSTON, BOTH BLACK AND WHITE, GATHERED AT ANTISLAVERY MEETINGS. IN THE YEARS BETWEEN THE REVOLUTIONARY WAR AND THE CIVIL WAR, MANY PEOPLE IN THE NORTH BEGAN TO PROTEST THE PRACTICE OF ENSLAVING HUMAN BEINGS. SLAVERY WAS FINALLY ABOLISHED IN 1865.

AFRICAN AMERICANS AND ABOLITIONISTS CELEBRATED
WHEN THE 13TH AMENDMENT BECAME LAW IN DECEMBER
OF 1865. BUT ALTHOUGH SLAVES WERE LEGALLY FREE,
BLACK AMERICANS WOULD CONTINUE TO STRUGGLE FOR
EQUAL RIGHTS FOR MANY YEARS TO COME.

Timeline

Year	Event	Year	Event
1766	Jenny Slew, an African American woman, wins her freedom in a Massachusetts court case.	*1779*	Thousands of southern slaves run away to work for the British, who promise them freedom.
1773–1774	Massachusetts slaves petition the court for their freedom. Their petitions are turned down.	*1780*	Pennsylvania abolishes slavery on March 1.
1775	Americans fight the British in the Battle of Lexington and Concord on April 19 and the Battle of Bunker Hill on June 17.	*1781*	In January, Americans defeat the British at the Battle of Cowpens.

1775

Americans fight the British in the Battle of Lexington and Concord on April 19 and the Battle of Bunker Hill on June 17.

In June, General Washington begins to exclude African Americans from the army.

1776

The 13 colonies accept the Declaration of Independence on July 4.

Prince Whipple helps row Washington's army across the Delaware River on Christmas Day. The next day, the Americans win the Battle of Trenton.

1777

General Washington begins to enlist African Americans in the army in January.

Vermont leaders outlaw slavery.

James Forten becomes a drummer boy in a militia unit in a Pennsylvania militia unit. He serves only for a short time.

1778

The British invade the southern colonies.

1779

Thousands of southern slaves run away to work for the British, who promise them freedom.

1780

Pennsylvania abolishes slavery on March 1.

1781

In January, Americans defeat the British at the Battle of Cowpens.

James Armistead begins to spy for the French general, Marquis de Lafayette.

James Forten becomes a powder boy on the American privateer, the *Royal Louis*.

Elizabeth Freeman wins her freedom in a Massachusetts court.

The British surrender after the Battle of Yorktown on October 19.

1782

James Forten is released from a British prison ship and returns to his family in Philadelphia.

1783

The United States and Great Britain sign the Treaty of Paris on September 3. The United States is officially an independent nation.

1861–1865

America fights the Civil War. After four years of bitter warfare, the South surrenders in 1865.

1865

The 13th Amendment, which guarantees the freedom of African Americans, becomes law on December 18.

Glossary

abolished (uh-BALL-isht)
If something is abolished, it is stopped or ended. Vermont and Pennsylvania were two of the first states to abolish slavery.

African American (AF-rih-kun uh-MAYR-ih-kun)
An African American is a black American whose ancestors came from Africa. At least 5,000 African American men and boys served in the American army during the Revolutionary War.

aide (AYD)
An aide is an officer who is a secretary and an assistant to a general. General William Whipple was General Washington's aide.

amendment (uh-MEND-ment)
An amendment is an addition or a change, especially to the Constitution of the United States. The 13th Amendment abolished slavery in the United States.

ammunition (am-yew-NISH-en)
Ammunition is bullets, cannonballs, and other things that can be fired from guns and cannons. The Americans began to store ammunition before the Revolutionary War began.

artillery (arr-TILL-ur-ee)
The artillery is a branch of the army. Soldiers in the artillery fire cannons and other heavy weapons.

descent (dee-SENT)
A person of African descent has parents, grandparents, or other ancestors who came from Africa. Most slaves were born in Africa or were of African descent.

earthworks (ERTH-werkz)
Earthworks are structures made out of mud and dirt. Earthworks protected American minutemen when British soldiers attacked.

Hessian (HEH-shen)
The Hessian soldiers were Germans hired by the British to fight the Americans during the Revolution. The Americans launched a surprise attack on Hessian troops at Trenton, New Jersey.

historians (hih-STOR-ee-unz)
Historians are people who study past events and why they happened. Some historians believe that women fought in the Revolutionary War.

independent (in-dee-PEN-dent)
If a country is independent, it is free to rule itself without interference from another country. The United States declared itself independent from Great Britain in 1776.

infantry (IN-fen-tree)
The infantry is a branch of the army. Soldiers in the infantry fight on foot and carry their own weapons.

Loyalists (LOY-ull-ists)
The Loyalists were Americans who did not want independence from Britain. Loyalists attacked the home of Captain Huddy.

merchant ships (MER-chent SHIPZ)
Merchant ships are vessels used for carrying goods to be bought or sold. The *Royal Louis* captured a British merchant ship.

Glossary

militias (meh-LISH-uhz)
Militias are groups of soldiers that are not part of a regular army. Militias serve in an emergency.

minutemen (MIN-it-men)
The minutemen were soldiers who promised to fight at a minute's notice during the early days of the Revolutionary War. Peter Salem is the best-known African American minuteman.

muskets (MUS-kitz)
Muskets were the most common guns during the Revolutionary War period. Muskets look similar to modern rifles.

orderlies (OR-der-leez)
Orderlies are assistants to army and naval officers. Many African Americans served as orderlies during the Revolutionary War.

patriot (PAY-tree-et)
A patriot was an American colonist who wanted independence from Britain. Crispus Attucks was an African American patriot.

petition (peh-TISH-un)
A petition is a written request or demand. A petition often is made by more than one person.

private (PRY-vit)
A private is a soldier of the lowest rank. African American soldiers were usually privates in the Revolutionary War.

privateer (pry-vuh-TEER)
A privateer is a war ship owned by a private citizen. The *Royal Louis* was a privateer.

rations (RASH-unz)
Rations are a person's share of food. Some free black men joined the army for the wages and food rations.

rebellion (ree-BELL-yun)
A rebellion is a fight against the government or its leaders. Slave owners worried that slaves would start a rebellion if they had weapons.

retreat (ree-TREET)
If an army retreats, it moves back or withdraws to avoid danger or defeat. The British were forced to retreat from their first attack at the Battle of Bunker Hill.

seized (SEEZD)
If people or things are seized, they are captured or taken by force. Jenny Slew, a free African American, was seized and forced into slavery.

traitor (TRAY-tur)
A traitor is a person who betrays his or her country. Traitors help their country's enemies.

tyranny (TEER-uh-nee)
Tyranny is a condition in which a government has absolute power and uses it unfairly or harshly. American patriots accused Great Britain of tyranny.

War for Independence (WAR FOR in-dee-PEN-dentz)
The War for Independence is the Revolutionary War. It is also called the American Revolution.

West Indies (WEST IN-deez)
The West Indies are islands in the Atlantic Ocean between Florida and South America. The West Indies allowed slavery and were controlled by the British.

Index

Further Information

Books

Cox, Clinton. *Come All You Brave Soldiers: Blacks in the Revolutionary War.* New York: Scholastic Press, 1999.

Davis, Burke. *Black Heroes of the American Revolution.* New York: Harcourt, 1992.

Meltzer, Milton. *The American Revolutionaries: A History in Their Own Words 1750–1800.* New York: HarperTrophy, 1987.

Murphy, Jim. *A Young Patriot: The American Revolution as Experienced by One Boy.* New York: Clarion Books, 1996.

Young, Alfred F., and Terry J. Fife with Mary E. Janzen. *We the People: Voices and Images of the New Nation.* Philadelphia: Temple University Press, 1993.

Web Sites

Learn more about African American minutemen:
http://www.ilt.columbia.edu/k12/history/blacks/blacks4.html

Learn more about the history of black soldiers in America:
http://www.coax.net/people/lwf/aa_mh.htm

Visit links to other sites about African American soldiers and heros:
http://www.coax.net/people/lwf/default.htm

Learn more about the American Revolution:
http://www.cgps.org/sgslab/colonialresources.htm